Introduction

To my nephew Joe

Magic Sparkles have been used the cakes in this book. They are edible and safe to use on any c
They can be used on cakes, sweets, chocolates or desserts for a special touch.
 Use straight from the pot or grind down to a finer glitter. To do this, either leave in the pot and
mortar. To attach to cakes the surface should be tacky not wet - if too wet they will dissolve. Ed can
use water or alcohol. Their appearance is enhanced by good lighting - halogen or spotlights work well.

How To Use The Size Guide (CC)

On any instructions for modelling in this book I have used the Cel Cakes Size Guide. This should make it easier to produce proportioned figures. To achieve the correct size, the ball of paste should sit in the correct hole (size below it) with 1/3 of the paste showing out of the bottom and 2/3 out of the top (this does not apply to the smallest sizes). You will then have approximately the correct size ball of paste to shape.

Recipes

Modelling Paste

Either:-$1/2$ sugarpaste, $1/2$ flower paste kneaded together, or knead 5ml (1tsp) of gum tragacanth into 225g (8ozs) sugarpaste and leave for 8 hours, or knead 5ml (1tsp) Tylo (CMC) powder into 225g (8ozs) sugarpaste.

Mexican Paste

Mix together 225g (8ozs) of icing sugar and 3 level teaspoons of gum tragacanth. Add 25ml (5tsp) of cold water (taken from tap). Mix together, turnout and knead well. Store in a plastic bag and a sealed container for 6-8 hours to mature. The paste will feel very hard but will soften up easily. Break off small pieces and soften in your fingers. Matured paste will freeze.

Royal Icing

Place 30ml (6 level tsp) of merriwhite in a mixing bowl and gradually add 5tbs cold water mixing with a wooden spoon until free from lumps. Add 225g (8ozs) of icing sugar and mix until smooth. Add 110g (4ozs) of icing sugar and then add the rest gradually until the correct consistency is reached. Beat well for approximately 5 minutes. Store in the fridge, in an airtight container. It should keep for 4 weeks.

Softened Sugarpaste

Place the amount of sugarpaste you want to soften in a bowl. Chop up roughly and then gradually add drops of cold water. Break down with a fork or a spoon and mix until smooth and lump free. Continue until required consistency is reached. The first time you do this, be careful not to add too much water too soon. It softens quickly.

Edible Glue

This is easily made with 1 part Tylo (CMC) powder to 25-30 parts water. Place the powder in a bottle or jar that has a lid. Add the water, replace the lid and shake. There will be thick creamy white pieces in the water. They will dissolve and the liquid will become clear by the following day.

NOTE: **ANY SPECIAL EQUIPMENT USED HAS A SUPPLIER CODE. FOR EXAMPLE – SIZE GUIDE (CC) – SUPPLIER CEL CAKES. SEE ACKNOWLEDGMENTS PAGE 37 .**

Bethlehem

20cm x 15cm (8 x 6in) Oval marzipanned rich fruit cake, 30.5cm x 25.5cm (12 x 10in) oval cake board, 1.3kg (3lb) Celebration Regalice, 50g (2oz) natural coloured marzipan, 250g (8oz) Atlantic Blue Regalice, 250g (8oz) Mexican paste, CMC (Tylo) powder, soft brown sugar, gold Magic Sparkles ground finer (see p1) (JK), a little royal icing, edible glue (p1), isopropyl alcohol, Trex.

Paste Colours: Bulrush (SK), Spruce Green, Paprika, Pink, Black (SF).

Powder colours: Brilliant Gold, Bulrush, Silver, Holly/Ivy, Moonbeams Jade (SK), Dusky Pink (SF).

Buildings cutter and star cutters from Shepherd set (PC), foliage cutters from Dinosaur set (PC), mouth embosser - veining tool (Jem), dresden tool, fine paintbrush, no.1 piping nozzle, two pieces of size 26 or 28 wire, non stick rolling pin and board, sponge pad, size guide (CC), sieve, a piece of strong card (at least 20cm x 10cm), circle cutters - 12cm & 8cm diameters.

1 Colour 200g of Mexican paste brown, but roll the paste and fold to distribute the colour to give a wood effect when rolled out. Roll out into a long strip 4mm thick. Cut two pieces measuring 5cm x 9cm and one piece 19cm x 6cm. Place side pieces on a sponge pad and roof piece over folded strong card. Place the card between two tins to prevent it opening flat. Leave to dry.

2 Cut four pieces of wire each 11cm. Twist all four together and curve slightly but leave 2.5cm at one end and open out so wires form a cross. Knead the brown colour into the Mexican paste trimmings so it is streak free. Roll small balls, flatten slightly then thread onto wires down to base. Paint a little glue between each piece. Continue until 2cm from top. Leave to dry.

3 Grease a non stick rolling board and building cutter with trex. Roll out brown Mexican paste thinly. Cut out buildings and separate with a knife. You will need approximately ten. Leave to dry on a sponge pad. Colour a little Mexican paste yellow and cut out 1 large star and 16 small. Leave to dry.

4 Colour some Mexican paste green and cut out 5 palm trees. When dry dust tree trunks with brown powder colour. Using the foliage cutters from the dinosaur set cut out 15 small and 5 medium for tree tops. Cut 4 of the medium in half. Leave to dry.

5 Ice board and cake. Place cake on board towards top left side 2cm from edge. Roll out a long strip of dark blue sugarpaste and cut to 5.5cm wide. Attach around cake side. Cut out buildings in Mexican paste as before but do not separate. Attach to cake with palm trees between. Attach small stars. Mix isopropyl alcohol with gold powder and paint stars. Use a fine paintbrush to paint tiny stars directly onto blue sugarpaste. Paint all building windows gold.

6 Dust edges of all palm tree tops dark green and centres with jade. Colour a little royal icing brown and pipe between sections of tree trunk on wires. Spread icing with a damp paintbrush. Attach small balls of green Mexican paste to tree tops around cake using royal icing coloured green. Attach small tree tops over. Pipe a line of brown royal icing along bottom edge of separate buildings and press into icing on board.

7 Cut out one more tree top with medium cutter. Brush the whole dried tree top cut out previously with glue and place against wires at top of the tree trunk. Position the soft piece the other side of wires and gently press tree tops together. Lay on side then pipe green royal icing down centre of tree top. Place tree half tops into this icing with small pieces of foam between to support. Leave to dry. Do not remove supports, turn over tree and repeat. Leave to dry. Cut a cross on iced board with a knife for wires to sink into, pipe a little royal icing under tree then push wires into icing. Pipe over with royal icing and cover with brown sugar for sand.

CONTINUED...

8 Mix a little of the dark blue sugarpaste into white and using the size guide (see p1) shape a cone from a size 15 ball of paste. Add a pinch of tylo powder to a size 15 ball of dark blue paste. Knead well and roll out to a circle with a diameter of 12cm. Cut out a $\frac{1}{2}$ of the circle then try the $\frac{1}{2}$ piece over the body for size. Alter if necessary then attach with glue.

9 Add a touch of pink and paprika paste colours to 25g of natural marzipan to give a flesh colour. Roll two tiny balls of marzipan for hands. Pinch and make a point on each. Use the dark blue paste trimmings with the tylo added to roll a size 11 ball. Roll into a sausage then cut in half diagonally to give the sleeve shape. Thin a little at shoulders, then make a hole at top of sleeve opening with a paintbrush handle for the hand. Brush each hole with a little glue then insert hand and bend upwards. Brush one hand with glue and sides of body. Stick hands together then lift both sleeves together and attach to body. Mark creases at elbows with a dresden tool.

10 Roll a size 12 ball of flesh coloured marzipan for head and attach with glue. Emboss mouth with tool. Dust cheeks with pink powder. Mark eyes with the tip of a cocktail stick dipped in black paste colour. Knead a small pinch of tylo powder into a ball of light blue sugarpaste. Roll out thinly and cut out a $\frac{1}{2}$ circle with a diameter of 8cm. Check for size over head, then brush with glue and attach. Colour a small piece of sugarpaste brown and soften with water (see p1). Place in a piping bag with a no.1 nozzle and pipe hair.

11 Before making Joseph, colour a little piece of Mexican paste darker brown and roll into a long thin stick measuring 6cm. Curve at one end and leave to dry. Repeat Mary instructions but omit the $\frac{1}{2}$ circle over body, bend Joseph's arms into different positions and attach crook under one hand. Make his headdress a little longer and attach a thin headband. Pipe beard and hair but make a little rougher with a damp paintbrush.

12 Colour some Mexican paste brown, folding as before for wood effect. Make four small blocks each 1cm square. Shape a piece 4.5 x 2cm and 1cm deep. Hollow out on top but keep oblong shaped. Attach to blocks with glue. Push small piece of marzipan through a sieve for straw. Cut off with a knife and attach around edge of manger.

13 Roll a tiny piece of white Mexican paste into a thin sausage and shape into a tiny halo. From a size 7 ball of white Mexican paste shape into an oval and brush glue on one side. Roll out a thin strip of Mexican paste 10-12cm long. Cut edges straight and to a width of 5mm. Attach one end to the glued side then roll around body. Make small hands and arms and attach. Roll a small ball of marzipan for head and attach with body to manger. Attach halo, dust cheeks, emboss mouth, mark eyes as before and pipe three little spikes of hair. Paint halo silver by mixing silver powder colour with isopropyl alcohol.

14 Paint large star with glue and cover with gold sparkles. Pipe a little royal icing under Mary, Joseph and Jesus and attach to top of cake. Spread some brown sugar around them. Pipe brown royal icing along bottom edges of stable sides and push into cake - they may need support with sponge until dry. When dry pipe royal icing along top edges of sides and position roof. Attach star with royal icing.

Reindeer and Mistletoe

20.5cm (8in) Marzipanned rich fruit cake, 28cm (11in) cake board, 700g (1_ lbs) Atlantic Blue Regalice, 900g (2lb) white sugarpaste, 2 pots White Magic Sparkles (JK), edible glue (see p1), royal icing, flower paste.

Paste Colours: **Bulrush, Black (SK), Red Extra, Spruce Green (SF).**

Powder Colours: **Bulrush, Black (SK), Red Extra, Spruce Green (SF).**

Small holly cutter from plunger set of 3 (PME), veining tool / mouth embosser (JEM), no.1,2 and 4 piping nozzles, paintbrush.

1 Place cake on board. Cover the top 13cm of the cake with Atlantic Blue Regalice. Cover the remaining cake with white sugarpaste. Ice the board with the appropriate colours to match the cake. Brush white icing with edible glue and cover with Magic Sparkles.

2 Soften white sugarpaste and place in a piping bag (see p1) with a no.2 piping nozzle. Pipe a small plain shell onto white icing around base of cake. Repeat with the blue.

3 Colour 280g of sugarpaste brown. Remove 20g for ears, tails and hooves. Divide the 260g into four equal pieces. Shape two bodies and two heads then attach. Emboss closed eyes with the mouth embosser.

4 Colour a little royal icing brown to match bodies. Place in a piping bag with a no.4 piping nozzle and pipe legs. Trace antler pattern from p32 then mark onto cake above heads with a cocktail stick. Soften the brown royal icing with a little water and add more paste colour to darken. Place in a piping bag with a no.2 nozzle and pipe antlers.

5 Roll balls of brown sugarpaste for ears, point and make teardrop shaped then hollow out with a paintbrush handle. Dust inside with a little pink powder colour then attach over antlers. Take two balls of sugarpaste, colour one red and the other black. Roll into oval shapes and attach to reindeer. From a small ball of sugarpaste shape a pointed tail and attach. Shape eight oval balls of sugarpaste for hooves. Mark with a knife and attach.

6 Colour some flower paste green. Cut out 4 holly leaves and attach to heads. Colour a little flower paste red, roll tiny berries and attach. From small balls of green flower paste, make teardrop shapes, flatten slightly and attach to antlers for mistletoe leaves. Place white royal icing in a bag with a no.1 nozzle and pipe various size bulbs of icing all over blue sugarpaste for snow.

20cm (8in) Rich fruit cake marzipanned and iced in Celebration Regalice on a 28cm (11in) iced cake board, Mexican paste, royal icing, edible glue, isopropyl alcohol, red Magic Sparkles ground finer (see p1), white Magic Sparkles (JK).

Paste Colours: Red Extra, Egg Yellow, Spruce Green (SF).

Powder Colours: Brilliant Gold, Holly/Ivy (SK).

Cutting Wheel, no.1 & no.2 piping nozzles, sponge pad, fine paintbrush.

1 Trace sleigh pattern from p33. Colour some Mexican paste red, roll out and use a cutting wheel to cut out the sleigh. Leave to dry on a sponge pad.

2 Colour some Mexican paste red and some cream using the yellow paste colour. Roll out thinly and cut out approximately 30-40 square and oblong shapes for parcels measuring between 1.5cm and 4cm in size. Keep 5-7 for top of cake and attach others around side of cake with edible glue.

3 Using the tracing, mark the sleigh legs and runners with a sharp knife or cocktail stick. Colour a little royal icing pale yellow and place in two piping bags, one with a no.1 nozzle, the other with a no.2 nozzle. Pipe the curved legs from the sleigh base to the runner with the no.1 nozzle and the runners with the no.2 nozzle. Over pipe the runners with the no.2 nozzle. The curves at the top left and right of the sleigh are also piped with the no.2 nozzle.

4 Brush sleigh thinly with glue. Cover with red sparkles. Colour some sugarpaste pale yellow. Roll out sausages and attach to top and bottom edges of sleigh. Mix isopropyl alcohol with gold powder and paint sleigh runners, legs and trims. Leave to dry. Brush a little glue onto cake under runners and add white sparkles.

5 Dust or paint a few of the yellow parcels gold Mix isopropyl alcohol with powder colours and paint small designs (holly, stars,

trees etc) on parcels around cake sides and the parcels for the top. Turn sleigh over. Roll small balls of sugarpaste and attach to sleigh with royal icing. Pipe a little royal icing onto each ball of paste then turn over and place on cake. Attach parcels into sleigh. Using red, yellow and green royal icing with no.1 an 2 nozzles, pipe ribbons, loops and bows. When dry, paint the yellow piping gold as before.

Teddy Santa

900g (2lb) Poppy Red Regalice, teddy bear cake and small teddy bear cake (see below), 30.5cm (12in) cake board, 1.6kg (3lb 8oz) sugarpaste, flower paste, royal icing, white Magic Sparkles ground finer (see p1) (JK), edible glue (P1), apricot jam, isopropyl alcohol, glycerine (optional) add 5ml to 450g of royal icing.

Paste Colours: Spruce Green, Red Extra, Dark Brown, Black (SF).

Powder Colours: White, Black, Moonbeams Jade and Ruby (SK), Dusky Pink (SF).

Cake tins - Wilton cake tins - stand up cuddly bear and mini stand up bear (PME), Wilton nozzle no.233 plus piping bag and adaptor (PME), Dresden tool, mini holly embosser from mini holly, ivy & mistletoe set (PC), veining tool / mouth embosser (JEM), size guide (CC), ball tool, paintbrushes.

1 Check the quantity of sponge cake mixture you usually use with the tin size. Do this by filling each half of the teddy tins with water and then pouring into you cake tins to see what size mix you will need. Follow the instructions given with the tins on how to use and bake.

2 Using the size guide (see p1), colour enough flower paste brown for 2 size 12 pieces. Roll each into a sausage with one end wider. Flatten the wider end slightly then cut out V shapes to shape antlers. Smooth the cut edges and leave to dry.

3 Colour approximately 700g (1½lbs) of sugarpaste green and ice board. Emboss with mini holly. Mix isopropyl alcohol with jade powder and paint leaves. Repeat with ruby to paint berries.

4 Trim arms off both cakes. Trim ears off large teddy. Colour approximately 700g (1½lbs) of sugarpaste brown. Cover both

cakes with apricot jam. Cover large teddy's head and small teddy with brown sugarpaste. On small teddy indent ears and eyes with the ball tool. Mark mouth with the Dresden tool and mouth embosser. Indent large teddy's eyes with the ball tool. Roll out 2/3rds of the red sugarpaste into a C shape measuring 46cm long lengthways down centre of cake and 13cm wide. Starting at the back of the teddy, wrap around body. Fit neatly at the neck and take excess underneath teddy. Trim straight at back join. Place cake on board towards back.

5 Colour 170g of sugarpaste black. Reserve a size 8 piece for nose and enough for eyes. Divide the remaining paste for feet, smooth into oval shapes and attach. Use the Dresden tool to mark heel. Roll sausages of white sugarpaste long enough for fur trimmings around jacket and trousers. Check size then attach with edible glue.

6 Take 60g of red sugarpaste for each arm, roll into sausages, flatten and attach to sides of body with edible glue. Attach a ball of brown sugarpaste to end of each sleeve for paw. Roll out remaining red sugarpaste and cut out a half circle with a diameter of 45cm.

Wrap around head for hat. Fold top point down to one side and secure with a little glue. Shape two ears from a size 12 ball of sugarpaste by flattening slightly, hollowing out with a ball tool and then cutting in half. Brush with pink powder colour then attach to hat with a little glue. Brush pink powder to both teddies cheeks and small teddy's ears and feet.

7 Mix isopropyl alcohol with black powder and paint large teddy's mouth. Roll small balls of black sugarpaste for eyes. Attach eyes and noses to both teddies with a little glue.

8 Soften white sugarpaste with water (P1) and place in a piping bag. Trim end and pipe over white fur trims. Use a damp paintbrush to pull out and 'stipple'. While damp cover with Magic Sparkles.

9 Colour some royal icing brown. Using the piping bag, adaptor and nozzle start to pipe the small teddy's fur. Do not have the icing too soft or overfill the piping bag. Practise first on some spare sugarpaste. Start to squeeze the icing out a little and touch to the cake. Squeeze a little more then stop before pulling away from cake. Start at the back of large teddy's head working from bottom to top, side to side. Cover head, ears, paws, and edge of feet.

10 Attach trims to hat and a bobble. Make sure the fur is dry before using softened sugarpaste and sparkles as before.

11 Add small teddy's arms each shaped from size 12 pieces of sugarpaste. Royal icing for small teddy can be lighter in colour. Pipe as before but pipe back of teddy and then place on cake board before continuing at front. Push dried antlers into top of head.

Let it Snow

20cm (8in) Round rich fruit cake, marzipanned and covered with sugarpaste coloured pale blue with Gentian paste colour (SK), 30.5cm (12in) cake board, 1kg (2lb 4oz) sugarpaste, a little royal icing, flower paste, edible glue (p1), isopropyl alcohol, 2 pots of white Magic Sparkles ground finer (see p1) (JK).

Paste Colours: Gentian, Marigold, Rose, Violet, Mint, Bluebell, Black (SK), Paprika (SF).

Powder Colours: Snowflake Lustre, White (SK).

Moulds are now available for the snowmen faces from cake decorating shops or visit our website.
Snowman head moulds (KD) or bone tool, mouth embosser (Jem), sieve, assorted crimpers, quilting tool (PME), cutting wheel (PME), fine paintbrush, dusting brush, no.1 piping nozzle, 7.5cm diameter circle cutter, pastry brush, greaseproof paper.

1 Place cake on board and using a pastry brush cover thinly and evenly with edible glue. Place over a sheet of greaseproof paper that has been folded in half and opened. Cover with magic sparkles and leave to dry for an hour. Using a soft dusting brush, remove excess gently then lift cake off paper. Tap sparkles into fold of paper then pour back into a pot. Brush glue around cake board. Roll out a long strip of white sugarpaste attach to board, trim and smooth cut edge with fingers.

2 Cut a strip of greaseproof paper to fit around side of cake. Measure and divide equally into twelve. Place around cake and mark positions for heads halfway up the cake side. Using approximately 45-50g of sugarpaste for each head, roll into a smooth ball then flatten for the face. Attach to side of cake between markings with glue. Use the smallest end of the bone tool to make a small indentation for nose in the centre of the face. Repeat for eyes. Use the round cutter to emboss a mouth and then the mouth tool at each side of mouth. Use a dusting brush to cover heads and covered board with snowflake lustre.

3 Colour some flowerpaste black. Roll small balls for eyes, flatten slightly, brush eye hollow with glue and place in position. Flatten and smooth eye surface further with finger. Mix a little white powder colour with water and paint a small light reflection to each eye.

4 Colour some sugarpaste in several colours. Cut out hats with a circle cutter (approximately 7.5cm diameter) and cut in half (you may need to trim further or stretch a little to fit). Attach with glue. Mark with either a dresden tool, stitch wheel or crimpers. Make each hat different to the one next to it. You can make tassles with small pieces of sugarpaste or bobbles by first attaching a ball of sugarpaste to the hat, then push small pieces of sugarpaste through a sieve and trim off with a knife. Brush bobble with glue, take the knife to the bobble and push strands of paste off knife onto bobble with a cocktail stick. Make scarves, bows etc from sugarpaste using the same tools.

5 Colour some flowerpaste orange with the paprika paste colour. Roll a small ball then pinch and roll to make a carrot shape. Mark fine lines randomly around sides with a knife. Bend slightly to point upwards and attach to face with a little glue.

6 Using a no.1 piping nozzle and royal icing, pipe the words 'let it snow' to the top centre of the cake. Pipe bulbs of icing for snow in various sizes. Leave to dry then paint over writing and snow using a isopropyl alcohol mixed with snowflake lustre.

Baby's 1st Christmas

18cm (7in) Marzipanned rich fruit cake - measured side to opposite side, 28cm (11in) cake board, 900g (2lb) sugarpaste, 225g (8oz) natural coloured marzipan, 2 pots of white Magic Sparkles (grind half a pot finer - see p1), 1 red Magic Sparkles ground finer (JK), a little royal icing, edible glue, flower paste.

Paste Colours: **Red Extra, Black, Paprika, Pink (SF).**

Powder Colours: **Dusky Pink (SF), Bulrush, Black, Snowflake Lustre (SK).**

Sleeping baby mould (SC), Teddy bear mould (FMM), no.1 piping nozzle, fine paintbrushes, mini holly embosser from Holly/Ivy/Mistletoe set (PC), small teddy from Make a Cradle set (PC), mini embossing stick from Micro Designs set 5 (HP), 2cm double curve serrated crimper, Dresden tool, size guide (see p1 on how to use), small scissors.

1 Place cake on board and cover with sugarpaste. Emboss randomly all over cake with the holly, teddy and mini embosser. Dust cake all over with snowflake lustre. Ice board and crimp edge. Cover iced board with edible glue and cover with magic sparkles. Pipe a small plain shell around base of cake using a no.1 nozzle and royal icing.

2 To make the teddies, knead small balls of marzipan and press into mould. Trim away excess. Release from mould and cut off left ear. Leave to dry. Make 6 teddies. Dust teddies paws, bottom of feet and inside ear with pink powder. Dust brown powder over bear avoiding pink areas and snout. Dust finely with snowflake. Use a fine paintbrush to paint eyes with black powder mixed with isopropyl alcohol. Paint nose and mouth with brown powder. Mix a little red paste colour with water to paint bow. Cover bow with red sparkles before it dries. Colour flower paste red and cut out a small triangle for hat. Attach with edible glue and tilt to the left. Mark creases with a knife. Brush lightly with edible glue and cover with red sparkles. Add a white fur trim and bobble from sugarpaste, brush lightly with glue and cover with fine white sparkles.

3 Using the size guide, measure two size 13 balls of marzipan. Colour flesh using a little paprika and pink paste colours. From this make two carrot shapes. Starting with the wide end at the head, press one piece into each mould. Trim away any excess with a knife. Turn moulds over, pull back sides and flick sharply to remove marzipan. Stick baby together with edible glue and leave to dry. Dust cheeks, paint lips, hair, eyebrows and closed eyelids.

4 Trace patterns on p34. Roll out red flower paste thinly and cut out baby's suit. Cover baby's body thinly with glue and place red suit over. Wrap around baby and take excess paste underneath. Trim paste over baby's bottom with scissors. Mark creases from tummy and backs of knees with a dresden tool. Cut out hat and brush head with a little glue. Wrap hat around head, folding point forwards and securing with glue. Colour a small piece of sugarpaste black. Shape two flattened ovals from this and attach over feet. Roll sausages of sugarpaste and attach around ankles, wrists, back of neck then face. Add a bobble to the hat.

5 Soften a little sugarpaste with water (see p1) and place in a piping bag. Pipe onto white trims and bobble. Use a damp paintbrush to spread out then cover with sparkles before sugarpaste dries.

6 Roll out some sugarpaste and cut out a 13cm diameter circle. Attach to top of cake. Dust plaque with snowflake. Colour a little royal icing red and place in a piping bag with a no.1 nozzle. Divide outside edge of circle into three. Pipe the words 'Baby's 1st Christmas' three times. Attach baby and teddies with royal icing.

Angel's Tree

Rich fruit cake baked in a 1.2 litre pudding bowl, 2 x 7.5cm (3in) fruit cakes, 1 large muffin cake, 30.5cm (12in) cake board, apricot jam, 900g (2lb) marzipan, 1.8kg (4lb) sugarpaste, rice paper, royal icing, edible glue (see p1), 1 x white magic sparkles ground finer (p1), 2 x hint of green Magic Sparkles (JK), 250g (9oz) flower paste, isopropyl alcohol, a little gin or vodka.

Paste Colours: Spruce Green, Paprika, Pink, Brown, Black (SF).

Powder Colours: Silver, White, Moonbeams Jade, Chestnut, Snowflake (SK), Dusky Pink (SF).

Large watermark taffeta rolling pin (HP), small star cutter (FMM), 2cm double curve serrated crimper, small holly cutter from plunger set (PME), mini holly embosser from Holly, Ivy & Mistletoe set (PC), Dresden tool, mouth embosser - veining tool (Jem), fine paintbrush, soft dusting brush, no.1 piping nozzle, Wilton piping nozzle no.233 plus piping bag and adaptor (PME), size guide (CC), satay stick, 4cm circle cutter, ball tool, wadding, sponge pad.

1 Colour a piece of flower paste grey. Roll out a sausage of paste 5mm thick and make a circle with a diameter approximately 7.5cm. From a very small ball of paste roll a sausage as thin as possible and make a circle with a diameter of 7mm. Leave both to dry. Roll out grey flower paste thinly and cut out 26 stars. From the same paste cut out 16 holly leaves. Soften the edges on a sponge pad and leave to dry.

2 Colour 700g of sugarpaste green and use to ice the board. Roll the taffeta rolling pin over then trim edges. Crimp around edge then dust with jade powder.

3 Trace wing patterns on p36. Use to cut out wings from rice paper. Brush large wings - one at a time, on one side only and very

thinly with edible glue. Cover with white sparkles. If curling up occurs, turn wings over to prevent.

4 Trim the narrow end of the pudding bowl cake so the angel is not too wide across her chest and shoulders. Brush with jam and cover with marzipan. Place cake on board, brush with vodka, roll out white sugarpaste quite thinly and cover.

5 Colour 350g of sugarpaste flesh using paprika and pink paste colours. Using the size guide take a size 15 ball of paste for each leg from this. Roll each leg into a sausage. At one end flatten and bend up for foot, mark with a Dresden tool and attach to cake with edible glue. Roll tiny balls of paste for toes in various sizes and attach starting with the smallest.

6 Mix together 200g each of flower paste and sugarpaste. Brush iced cake with vodka. Roll mixed paste into a circle large enough to cover cake. Trim edge neatly then crimp. Emboss around edge with holly embosser then crimp again above this. Lift over cake and adjust folds around hem of dress.

7 Roll two size 15 balls of white sugarpaste into a sausage. Cut in half diagonally across centre to give two shaped sleeves. Thin out and flatten slightly at each shoulder. Roll two size 10 balls of sugarpaste for hands. Pinch and make a point to push up sleeve then flatten slightly. Use a paintbrush handle to make a hole at top of each sleeve opening. Brush each hole with a little glue and the palm of one hand. Push hands into sleeves, push hands together. Brush glue thinly onto dress ready for arms. Lift both arms together and attach to cake.

8 Trim the muffin to a more rounded shape for head. Check size in comparison to body. If a little small you could either marzipan before icing, or roll out icing thicker than usual. Brush muffin with apricot jam then cover with flesh coloured sugarpaste. Keep the face area smooth and take excess paste to the back of head. Insert a satay stick through neck of dress down to board. It should protrude 5cm to attach the head, so remove and trim. Replace and attach head over. Indent for eyes with a ball tool and emboss mouth with a circle cutter and a mouth tool at each end.

9 Colour a little flower paste black. Roll small balls of black and white paste for eyes and attach. Roll a small ball of sugarpaste for nose and attach. Dust cheeks lightly with pink powder. Mix isopropyl alcohol with white powder to paint highlights in eyes. Use brown powder and a fine paintbrush to paint eyelashes and eyebrows.

10 Colour some royal icing brown and using the no.233 nozzle, adaptor and piping bag, pipe angel's hair. It is best to pipe the hair in layers and work your way around her head. Also pipe a fine fringe with a no.1 nozzle. Leave to dry for an hour then pipe a little icing onto back of large halo and press into hair. Tilt it by supporting with wadding until dry. Attach holly leaves and pipe small

CONTINUED...

berries. When dry mix silver powder with isopropyl alcohol and paint. Attach wings to angels back with white royal icing.

11 Brush top of one small fruit cake with jam then place the other on top. Trim to a cone shape then brush with jam and cover with marzipan keeping the top pointed. Colour 500g of sugarpaste green. Roll out to $1/2$ a circle. Brush tree with vodka and cover with green icing. Smooth excess icing to the top and point. Keep the join at the back and smooth. Place tree cake on board and brush thinly all over with glue. Cover with green sparkles and leave to dry. Use a soft brush to remove excess from tree then board. Paint stars silver and attach to tree with royal icing.

12 Take a size 9 piece of sugarpaste and roll into a cone shape. Hollow underneath at widest end with a paintbrush handle. Attach to tree with a little glue. Make two tiny teardrop shape hands. Roll a small sausage of sugarpaste for sleeves and cut in half diagonally. Use a cocktail stick to make small hole to push hands into securing with glue. Stick hands together then attach both sleeves to body. Roll a small ball of sugarpaste for head and attach. Cut a small mouth with a knife, dust cheeks, then mark eyes with the tip of a cocktail stick dipped in black paste colour. Pipe hair with the no. 1 nozzle. Attach halo and paint silver. Attach wings with royal icing. Brush small angel's dress and wings and large angel's dress with snowflake dust.

20cm (8in) Rich fruit cake, 28cm (11in) cake board, 1kg (2lb 4ozs) Celebration Regalice, flower paste, small piece of white sugarpaste, white and red Magic Sparkles (JK), edible glue (p1), a little royal icing (p1), isopropyl alcohol.

Paste Colours: **Spruce Green, Red extra, Egg Yellow, Dark Brown, Black (SF).**

Powder Colours: **Brilliant Gold, Ruby & Jade Moonbeams, Burnt Copper, Holly/Ivy, White (SK).**

No.1 piping nozzle, quilting tool (PME), cutting wheel (PME), small star cutter (FMM), small holly spray from Mini Holly, Ivy and Mistletoe set (PC), small holly plunger cutter from Holly plunger set (PME), bone tool, size guide (CC), sponge pad, paintbrush, greaseproof paper.

1 Place cake on board and cover with sugarpaste. Emboss around bottom edge of cake with the holly embosser. Ice board and emboss holly close to cake. Using flower paste and the plunger cutter, cut out approximately 86 holly leaves - plus some spare). Place on a sponge pad, soften edges with a dog bone and leave to dry.

2 On top of cake measure approximately 6.5cm down from top of cake on each side. Mark the centre for the washing line 10cm from top of cake. Place greaseproof paper over and mark these positions. Remove paper and draw a curve, cut along curve, place back over cake and mark line with a cocktail stick. Colour a little royal icing yellow and with a no.1 nozzle, pipe the washing line. Pipe a small curved line down at each end. Pipe the word 'Seasons' at the top and 'Greetings' at the bottom of the cake.

3 Colour some flower paste green and red. Trace and cut out the stocking patterns from p35. Cut out stockings, emboss stars or stripes with the dresden tool (opposite end of the stitch wheel). Use the stitch wheel on small green stocking and the dresden tool on large. First emboss toe and heel, then lines down the stocking, then the small markings.

Attach to cake with edible glue.

4 Colour a little flowerpaste yellow. Roll out to a thickness of 2mm and use the cutting wheel to cut long strips of paste. Cut into pegs measuring 1cm. Mark a line across using the Dresden tool.

5 Dust green stockings with Jade. Paint stars by mixing gold powder with isopropyl alcohol. Grind a little of the red Magic Sparkles finer (P1) and attach to red stocking with edible glue. Add a white sugarpaste trim to large green stocking and cover with white Magic Sparkles.

6 Attach pegs with a little royal icing. Mix isopropyl alcohol with gold powder and paint washing line, pegs and writing.

7 Colour some flowerpaste red and roll approximately 86 small balls. Dust embossed and cut out holly leaves with holly/ivy powder then jade powder. Attach holly leaves to each end of washing line, then alternatively up side of cake and then onto board using royal icing. Attach berries. Dust over berries with ruby.

8 Colour some sugarpaste brown. Roll small balls of paste for robin's tails, flatten and mark two lines for tail feathers. Attach under line. Using the size guide measure two size 11 balls of sugarpaste and colour red. Roll into a ball for each body, flatten slightly and attach to cake above washing line. Roll small balls of brown sugarpaste for wings each a size 7. Point and flatten slightly then attach to sides of bodies.

9 Roll a ball of sugarpaste size 9 for each head. Flatten slightly and attach. Dip the tip of a cocktail stick into brown paste colour and mark eyes. Colour a little flower paste black, shape into two small beaks and attach. Soften a little brown sugarpaste with water (P1) and brush onto robins with a damp paintbrush.

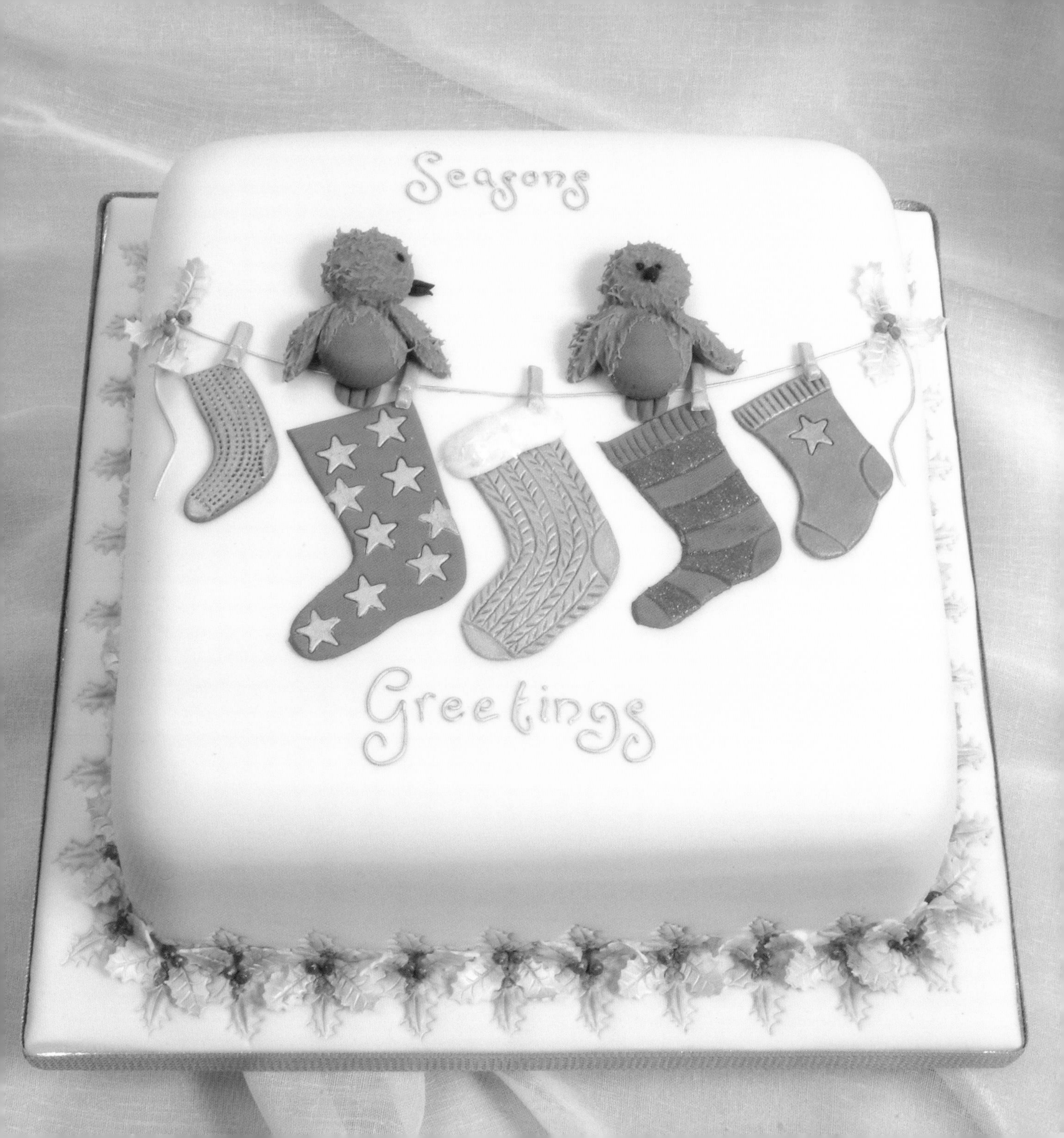
Seasons
Greetings

23cm (9in) Marzipanned Rich fruit cake (measured side to opposite side), 30.5cm (12in) cake board (side to side), 900g (2lb) sugarpaste, flower paste, edible glue, royal icing, 2 pots of white and 1 gold Magic Sparkles (JK), Isopropyl Alcohol, Mexican Paste, Trex.

Paste Colours: **Spruce Green, Egg Yellow (SF).**

Powder Colours: **Spruce Green, Egg Yellow (SF).**

Christmas tree cutter set of 3 (PME), large plaque cutter (PME), star cutters from Shepherd, Halloween or Angel Set (PC), paintbrush, no.1 & no.2 piping nozzles, non stick rolling pin and board, wadding or kitchen paper, sponge pad.

1 Place cake on board. Cover with sugarpaste and ice board. Remove a pinch of white sparkles from pot and keep for later. Grind remaining sparkles finer (see p1). Brush iced board with edible glue and cover with fine sparkles. Colour some royal icing pale yellow and place in a piping bag with a no.2 nozzle. Pipe a small plain shell around base of cake.

2 Colour some flower paste green. Roll out and cut out 6 large trees. Cut 5 in half. Cut out 15 small trees. Cut 9 in half. Colour a little Mexican paste yellow. Grease a non stick rolling board and star cutters with trex. Roll out Mexican paste thinly and cut out 1 large star, 7 small stars and 1 the next size to small. Leave stars and trees on a sponge pad to dry.

3 Roll out green flower paste thinly and cut out 7 plaques. Use the medium size Christmas tree cutter to cut a tree from the centre of six plaques. Dust all 7 plaques with jade powder. Attach whole plaque to cake centre and the six remaining to cake sides using royal icing.

4 Using the yellow royal icing and the no.2 nozzle, pipe the outlines to each plaque. Repeat piping a 2nd line directly on top. Use white royal icing and a no.1 nozzle to pipe the word 'Greetings' on centre plaque.

5 Brush one side of each tree piece with edible glue. Cover with the fine magic sparkles. Leave to dry. Turn over and repeat on other side. Colour a little royal icing green and attach whole small trees into the cut out tree in the plaques on the cake sides. Pipe a line of icing down the centre of each small tree and place a cut half directly onto piped line, then a half each side. Add more royal icing if needed and space tree halves evenly.

6 On the large tree, pipe a thick line of royal icing from top to bottom. This time attach a centre half, then two each side. They will need supporting with wadding or kitchen paper until dry. When dry stand tree up and attach tree halves on other side.

7 Mix isopropyl alcohol with gold powder colour. Paint plain shell, plaque edges and stars. Grind some gold sparkles finer. Sprinkle stars immediately after painting with gold sparkles. Attach large star to top of large tree, a small star to each tree on cake sides and 2 remaining stars to top of cake.

8 Spread a little royal icing roughly to the top left of plaque on top of cake. Cover with the large flake white magic sparkles. Pipe a little white icing under tree and position on top of cake.

Noel

20cm (8in) Marzipanned rich fruit cake, 28cm (11in) cake board, 1.2kg (2lb 12oz) sugarpaste, Mexican paste, edible glue (p1), a little royal icing, 2 x Red Magic Sparkles (JK).

Paste Colours: Red Extra (SF), Black, Bulrush (SK).

Dust Colours: Dusky Pink (SF)

1.7m Sheer gold ribbon, 1m white ribbon, glue stick, cutting wheel, small sharp knife, veining stick / mouth embossing tool (Jem), Dresden tool, bone tool, paintbrush, size guide (see p1) (CC), sponge pad.

1 Place cake on board and cover with sugarpaste. Colour approximately 200g of sugarpaste red and ice board. Attach gold ribbon around base of cake using royal icing.

2 Grind half a pot of sparkles finer (see p1). Brush iced board thinly with edible glue and cover with the large flake sparkles.

3 Trace 'Noel' pattern from p36. Colour some Mexican paste red. Roll out thinly and cut out each letter with a cutting wheel. Use a small sharp knife to cut into corners. Place on a sponge pad to dry.

4 Colour 240g of sugarpaste brown for the teddies. Using the size guide roll 4 size 14 balls of sugarpaste, shape into an oval and flatten slightly. Using edible glue, attach one to the left edge and one to the right edge on top of the cake. Check the position of the middle two bodies before attaching. Remember to keep enough space around each body to attach the arms.

5 Shape each leg from a size 11 piece of sugarpaste. Roll into a sausage shape, slightly wider at one end. At the wide end pinch out for the foot, flatten the sole and pinch a heel at the back. Thin the top of the leg a little and attach to body.

6 Each head is a size 11. Roll a ball and flatten slightly. Attach to cake. Roll a size 6 for each snout. Attach and emboss a mouth with the embosser. Mark a line in centre with a Dresden tool. Colour a small piece of Mexican paste black then shape and attach noses. Dip the tip of a cocktail stick into black paste colour and mark eyes. For ears roll size 6 balls of sugarpaste and flatten. Hollow out with a bone tool. Dust inside hollow with pink powder colour. Cut in half and attach to heads. Dust soles of feet and sides of snouts with pink.

7 Brush letters with edible glue. Cover with the fine sparkles. Remove excess sparkles by turning over and tapping gently. Soften some brown sugarpaste with water (see p1) and place in a piping bag. Pipe sugarpaste under the letter 'N' and place on top of teddy. Keep it as high up the teddy as possible. Shape arms each from a size 9 piece of sugarpaste and attach to teddy then letter. Repeat for each letter and teddy.

8 Pipe softened sugarpaste on to the first bear. Use a damp paintbrush to spread the icing out then 'stipple'. Repeat to each bear. Use a glue stick to attach white ribbon then gold ribbon around board.

Mini Cakes

Each cake is a 7.5cm (3in) rich fruit cake, marzipanned, iced and placed on a 15cm (6in) 4mm thick cake board.

Gold Tree
(iced in Celebration Regalice)

Small piece of Mexican paste, white Magic Sparkles (JK), edible glue, royal icing, isopropyl alcohol.

Paste Colours: **Egg Yellow (SF)**.

Powder Colour: **Brilliant Gold (SK)**.

Tree cutter (PME), Stars from shepherd set (PC)

1. Place cake on board and ice board with sugarpaste. Crimp around outside edge.

2. Grease a non stick rolling board and the star cutters with trex. Colour a little Mexican paste pale yellow and roll out thinly. Cut out one large star and 30 each of the two smallest size. Leave to dry. Colour a little sugarpaste pale yellow, cut out the tree and brush with gold powder colour.

3. Brush iced board with edible glue and cover with Magic Sparkles. Colour a little royal icing pale yellow and place in a piping bag with a no.1 nozzle. Attach tree to top of cake. Pipe around outside edge of tree and pipe small curls inside the tree. Attach the large star to the top. Attach remaining stars randomly around side of cake. Pipe a small plain shell around base of cake and overpipe the crimped edge.

4. Mix isopropyl alcohol with gold powder and paint stars and all piping. Add thin touches of glue to tree and add some Magic Sparkles.

Trees and Stars

Mexican or flower paste, 2 pots of white Magic Sparkles ground finer (P1) (JK), edible glue.

Paste Colours: **Mint Green, Violet, Rose (SK)**.

No.1 piping nozzle, small & medium Christmas tree cutters from set of 3 (PME), small star cutter (FMM), silver wires - size 26, smoother, posy pick.

1. Cut out approximately 15-20 small trees in pale green flower or Mexican paste. Attach to cake with a little edible glue. Press trees into cakes icing with a smoother. Ice cake board.

2. Soften a little sugarpaste (see P1) and place in a piping bag with a no.1 nozzle. Pipe a small plain shell around base of cake. Brush icing on board with glue and cover with sparkles.

3. Cut 4 silver wires in half. Cut out 16 medium trees in pale green flower paste. Brush 8 with glue and position a wire just over $1/2$ way up the centre of each. Place a tree directly on top. Leave to dry. Colour some flower paste pink and some lilac. Cut 3 silver wires in half. Roll out one colour and cut out 30 stars. Glue and position 5 stars from the top of each wire with a space of 1cm between each. Place a star on top of each. Repeat with the other colour. Brush one side of stars and trees with glue and cover with sparkles. Turn over and repeat.

4. Cut lengths of silver wire, wrap around a paintbrush handle and remove. Make five. Push a posy pick into the centre of the cake. Measure how much is showing above the cake. Remove posy pick and trim the pointed end as required. Push back into the cake. Fill the posy pick with Mexican or flower paste up to 1cm from the top. Push tree, stars and curly wires into paste in posy pick. Leave to dry then bend into position.

Winter Wonderland

1 Pot hint of blue and 2 pots white Magic Sparkles ground finer (see p1) (JK), a little royal icing, 200g (7oz) sugarpaste, isopropyl alcohol, edible glue (P1).

Paste Colours: **Black, Violet, Bluebell (SK)**.

Powder colours: **Silver, Snowflake Lustre (SK), Dusky Pink (SF)**.

No.1 piping nozzle, Dresden tool.

1. Ice board. Brush cake and board thinly with edible glue. Sprinkle a little of the Blue sparkles across top of cake. Cover cake and board with White sparkles.

2. Colour 30g of sugarpaste black. Remove small pieces and shape into teardrops for wings. Divide the black paste into $1/3$ and $2/3$. Shape into teardrop shapes and attach with wings to cake using edible glue. Cover front of teardrops with white sugarpaste. Dust a little pink powder onto cheek area. Colour a little sugarpaste grey and from this shape and attach two beaks. Dip the tip of a cocktail stick into black paste colour and mark eyes.

3. Colour one piece of sugarpaste lilac and one piece pale blue. Shape a hat from each and mark with a Dresden tool. Attach to penguins and add bobbles and fur trims.

4. Colour a little royal icing grey and place in a piping bag with a no.1 nozzle. Pipe penguin's legs. Shape boots for each penguin and attach. Add fur trims. Pipe the words 'Walking in a Winter Wonderland' around board. Pipe small snowflakes over cake.

5. Dust penguins (avoid black area) with snowflake. Mix isopropyl alcohol with silver powder and paint snowflakes and lettering.

20cm (8in) Marzipanned rich fruit cake, 30.5cm (12in) cake board, 900g 2lb Celebration Regalice, flower paste, royal icing, edible glue (see p1), gold Magic Sparkles ground finer (p1) (JK), isopropyl alcohol, confectioners varnish.

Paste Colours: Spruce Green, Egg Yellow, Red Extra (SF).

Powder Colours: Brilliant Gold, Holly/Ivy (SK).

Ivy plunger cutter set (PME), Holly plunger cutter set (PME), small pointed scissors, 2cm single curve serrated crimper, green reel wire or size 32 wires, size 26 wires, sponge pad, paintbrushes, rose leaf veiner, dresden tool, bone tool, white and green stemtex (florists) tape, black stamens, no.1 piping nozzle, posy pick.

1 Colour some flower paste dark green with the paste colour. Roll out small pieces thinly keeping a thicker central area to insert size 26 wire. Push wire half way into paste then cut out holly leaf and push down plunger. Place on a sponge pad and soften edges with a bone tool. You will need six in each size. When dry brush with confectioners varnish.

2 Colour some flower paste red. Roll 9 small balls and insert a black stamen in each but keep the tip visible. Leave to dry then dip into confectioners varnish and leave on polythene to dry.

3 Take half width tape and bind 3 berries close together. Add 2 small holly leaves above berries then 2 medium and 2 large below.

4 Colour some flower paste yellow and using ivy cutters, repeat instructions for holly leaves. You will need 6 of each size. When dry dust gold powder over back and front of leaves. Brush top of leaves only very thinly with edible glue. Cover with gold sparkles.

Tape together into sprays with 2 of each size leaf on each starting with the small.

5 Colour a small piece of flower paste yellow, a small piece pale green, a larger piece darker green and another large piece red. Cut 9 pieces of the fine wire to 7cm. Make a small hook at one end of each wire. Take a small ball of pale green and push it up the wire pulling the hook into the paste. Shape into a cone then cut small V shapes all over using the small scissors. Take a tiny piece of yellow paste and shape it into a leaf. Place on a sponge pad and mark a central vein with a Dresden tool. Secure to side of bud with a little glue. Repeat eight times.

6 Trace small leaf and the bract patterns from p32. Cut out 3 small pale green leaves and attach to fine wires. Vein with the rose leaf veiner, soften with a dog bone tool and leave to dry. Using red flower paste cut out 4 medium and 5 large bracts, plus 4 large bracts in green, inserting wires, veining and softening as before.

7 Dust edges of red and green bracts with gold powder colour. Mix isopropyl alcohol with gold powder colour and using a fine paintbrush, paint veins on all bracts. Paint veins on the small green leaves. Paint points on buds gold and the tiny green leaf at the side of each.

8 Tape poinsettia buds together in groups of 3. Next tape the 3 bunches of buds together. Add the 3 small green leaves evenly around centre buds. Bend the red bracts wire so they are at an angle of approximately 90 degrees. Starting with the smallest bract, tape to the buds, finally adding the green bracts. Tape the holly sprays around the poinsettia, then the ivy in between each holly spray.

9 Place marzipanned cake on board and cover with Celebration Regalice. Ice board. Crimp up front left corner of cake, over top edge and down right corner. Repeat at back of cake. Brush edible glue around base of

cake. Roll a long thin sausage of sugarpaste, attach around base of cake and crimp.

10 The cake can either have the writing as in the picture or if it looks difficult you could pipe the words 'Merry Christmas' towards the bottom right side of the cake top. To write all over the top and sides you first need to make a paper template in one piece of the top and two sides together. Fold the paper to find the centre line for writing, then measure three lines evenly either side. Pipe the words 'Merry Christmas on a spare piece of paper and measure. Now mark on your template the size of the lettering on each line leaving a gap of approximately 2.5cm between each. Make holes in the paper with a cocktail stick then lay over cake and mark lightly. Colour royal icing pale yellow and place in a piping bag with a no.1 nozzle. Pipe 'Merry Christmas all over top and sides of cake.

11 Colour a little royal icing red and overpipe crimping on cake with a no.1 nozzle. Use green icing to overpipe crimping around bottom edge of cake. Mix isopropyl alcohol with gold powder and paint all writing. Push posy pick into cake and position spray.

Christmas
Merry Christmas
Merry
Merry Christmas Merry
Christmas Merry Christmas
Merry Christmas Merry

Fern Wreath

20cm (8in) Marzipanned rich fruit cake, 30.5cm (12in) cake board, 1.1kg (2lb 8oz) sugarpaste, 225g (8oz) Mexican paste, 2 pots white Magic Sparkles ground finer (p1) (JK), edible glue (p3), Trex.

Paste Colour: Spruce Green (SF).

Powder Colour: Moonbeams Jade and Ruby (SK)

Fern leaf cutter (FMM), large holly plunger cutter (PME), large dusting brush, non stick rolling pin and board, dog tool, no.1 piping nozzle, kitchen paper, sponge pad.

1 Place cake on board. Colour sugarpaste green, ice cake then board. Soften a small piece of leftover sugarpaste with water (see p1) and place in a piping bag with a no.1 nozzle. Pipe a small plain shell around base of cake.

2 Grease a non stick rolling board with trex. Roll out Mexican paste thinly. Grease cutter and cut out several fern leaves at a time. While leaves are still on board, pick out pieces of paste between leaves with a cocktail stick, trim stem to half its length, remove excess paste, knead trimmings back together ready to use again. Place cut out leaves on pieces of flat kitchen paper to dry. You will need approximately 100 leaves but cut out 20 extra to allow for breakages.

3 Using Mexican paste cut out 16 holly leaves (3 for each corner plus 4 spare). Place on a sponge pad and soften edges with a ball tool. Roll 12 small balls of paste for berries and leave to dry.

4 Place Magic Sparkles in a bowl. Working on 10 at a time, brush fern leaves thinly with edible glue. Hold each leaf over bowl and sprinkle with the sparkles. Shake gently to remove excess and leave to dry.
Using the remaining sugarpaste roll out a

long sausage approximately 40cm long. Brush a circle glue on top of cake and place sugarpaste over this. Smooth sides of sugarpaste circle down towards cake.

6 Use a large dusting brush to cover cake and iced board with jade powder colour. Dust holly leaves with jade and berries with ruby. Attach to corners of cake on the board with soft sugarpaste or glue.

7 Start to push stem of fern leaves into sugarpaste circle. Work across from side to side and forward. Each leaf in next row should be positioned over gap between leaves of previous row. Sometimes this doesn't work out exactly but if you keep the leaves quite close together it won't be noticed. The outside edge of circle should have more leaves than the inner edge.

Patterns

Reindeer & Mistletoe Page 6

Poinsettia Cake Page 28

Small leaf

Large bract

Small bract

Sleigh Page 8

Patterns

Baby's 1st Christmas Page 14

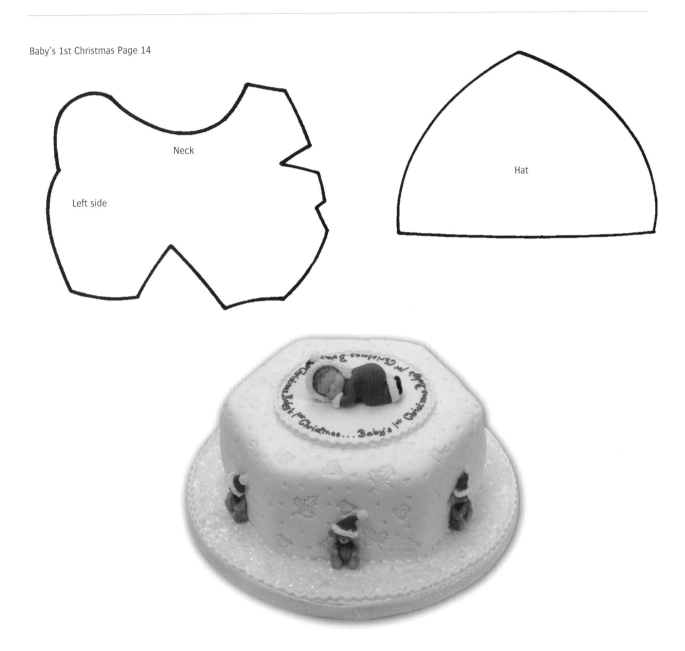

Neck

Left side

Hat

Stockings Page 20

Cut 2

Patterns

Actual size

Noel Page 24

Angel's Tree Page 16 - 19

5.4cm